Back to Yesterday

Zöe Broome

Back to Yesterday

Zöe Broome

Three Drops Press
Sheffield, England

First published in 2016 by Three Drops Press

Copyright © Zöe Broome 2016

All rights reserved. This book or any portion thereof may not be reproduced or used in any manner whatsoever without the express written permission of the publisher except for the use of brief quotations in a book review or scholarly journal.

Zöe Broome has asserted her right to be identified as the author of this book in accordance with the Copyright, Designs and Patents Act, 1988.

Three Drops Press
Sheffield, United Kingdom

www.threedropspoetry.co.uk

Three Drops Press is an independent imprint of Endaxi Press.

ISBN 978-1-907375-09-5

Book and cover design © Kate Garrett 2016

Aisling:

A poem, a girl, a woman, a dream

Formations	10
Cabin	11
Failed Pygmalion	13
Eroding	14
The Girl Garden	15
Do you Remember	16
The Tale of the Twig Girl	17
Turning Cinders	18
How We Lived Then	19
Come, My Scrabble Lover	20
Your Game of Cards	21
Your Game of Chess	22
Whitby	23
Anchored	24
Beware of nets –	25
Captured	26
Sea Girl	27
"Worse things happen at sea"	28
Our words	29
Persephone	30
Waiting for You	31
Rising from Ashes	32
Our love	33

When you wake	34
Why is it, when you	35
Of course, I	36
Announcing Ourselves	37
Tell me again	38
In this moment,	39
Our kiss, our kicks, our dance-floor skips,	40
Forgetting you	41
Rest	42
Shedding	43
Digital Aubade	44
Return to Our Island	45
Erosion	46
Apples	47
Toxic	48
Strange to think	49
Acknowledgements	51

Formations

"Remember that I am thy creature; I ought to be thy Adam, but I am rather the fallen angel."

- Mary Shelley, *Frankenstein*

Cabin

Another scattered track land.

You blatz a snowstorm
against rocks.

We forged a fort
on mountains:

our own snow-world.

Can you see snow
        d
         r
          i
           f
            t
                d
                o
                w
                n
                        ski-slopes?

Snug underfoot.

Reaching the bottom,
we'll climb

'til snow
       t
      u
        m
          b
            l
              e
                s

like rag blankets

& we
        collapse

                into
                          New
                                  Territory.

Failed Pygmalion

I chanced her in snow:

ice-blink skin,
hand-me-down hat.

In my arms,
she melted.

Eroding

Our beach flickers firelight,
New Year reaches shore.

A dog barks, warning:
'Remember last year,
December is only a day ago.'

I ignore. Backtrack to bonfires.

Cliffs crumble, consume ghosts I clung to,
slip into sea.

I supposed our salty town solid,
yet, when I return,
        it shifts –

a hotel's shut,
      or else,
            our land's lost.

The Girl Garden

"Fairies have to be one thing or the other, because being so small, they unfortunately have room for one feeling only at a time."

- J.M. Barrie, *Peter Pan*

Do you Remember

    our adventure
      between
climbing frames / bills

                             up
                 wracked
before words

& divided
day/dreams?

The Tale of the Twig Girl

We found the Twig Girl
by bushes
where fairies lived.

At night,
we dreamt she turned human
and danced on grass.

Later, we found her dead,

deprived of our dreams:
a stick-insect.

Turning Cinders

Scorched dawn,
dried-out moat.

Fairy-tale fields
secrete stories.

Princess,
do you hear roaring
in the lair?

In our silence,
growls echo.

Princess turns Cinders,
coach shrinks to pumpkin.

Moonlight freezes, now.

How We Lived Then

"We loved with a love that was more than love."

- Edgar Allan Poe, *Annabel Lee*

Come, My Scrabble Lover

Place your words of passion,
tally your points of love.
Come, my Scrabble lover,
play our game tonight.

Pick letters from my bag,
lay your triple word score.
Come, my Scrabble lover,
win our game tonight.

Your Game of Cards

In the old house,
you suggest a game of cards.

This game will reveal
who's king, jack and joker.

You keep the Queen of Hearts
in your back pocket.

Your Game of Chess

I whisper
"come to bed"
you sit over your chessboard.

"Aw, c'mon,
everyone knows chess"

It's your game, not mine.

I never learnt
to manoeuvre
your knights and bishops.

Whitby

Follow me down stony roads,
where jet shops, fudge shops, bookshops compete.

At midnight, we wake
to wind-whispers.

The black coated man
seeks his sleepwalking woman.

Everything repeats here,
here, everything repeats.

The cliffs' jaw-jags
bite into sea.

Anchored

Black and white ships
at the harbour.

Children skip with rope
from fishing boats. Their songs
haunt a candyfloss foreshore.

Boats are held back
by anchors
like I
am held back

from you.

Beware of nets —
mermaids
must never
get caught.

Captured

Today, you say
"love me": half-plea
half-order. You sense

this disturbance of sands

but take me

       anyway.

Sea Girl

i
Step barefoot where sands
tickle your toes.

Alone on a midwinter morning,
remember how to paddle.

Start swimming.

ii
You say
you were a fish
in a past life.

iii
And then (you tell me)
a mermaid.

I swim through ice,
chasing you
into sunlit sea.

iv
I follow your music

crash against your rock.

I see no tail.

You are no mermaid,
        I see your siren-smile.

"Worse things happen at sea"
they say

as if knowing
about shipwrecks
could cure heartache.

Our words
pitter patter:
tapping rain
before our storm.

Persephone

Come out with me
> *follow me home*

taste the sweet fruit
> *swallow its seeds*

let me hold you
> *grasp your body.*

Wake in springtime
> *go home again*

leave me alone
> *face her anger*

obey her words
> *full of her lies.*

Scamper on grass
> *she will chase you*

her 'pride and joy'
> *you'll break her heart*

sunlight will rise
> *will you be trapped?*

A new harvest
> *give me your crop*

her dying year
> *return to me*

as light draws in
> *Now! Escape, now!*

Waiting for You

I wait for your return
from the taverna.

I wasted my day
wrestling you,
trying to claim you
through our arguments.

Now,
you are gone.

Rising from Ashes

Brittle bones laid out on stone furnace,
from a bird who spent all winter dead,
stripped skull showing no face.

I remember I once heard it said
how high the bird flew, how well it could sing
on sunlit days, before the bird was dead.

Tell me - was it last summer or spring
we watched as we called out its name?
We saw it flutter each feather-filled wing.

My darling, burn it, because the shame
of a corpse reminds me: hope can't survive
so scatter its skull into hot flames.

I heard it call just now. Is it alive?
Its eyes shine like sunlight at dawn.
In this dead winter, can it survive?

Feather by feather, it's being reborn.

Our love

t
      u
            m
                b
                    l
                        e
                            s

(in) to

being –
Intense but *unsure* …

When you wake

I love your look:

amongst cake crumbs,
in your blue dressing gown

swallowed by your dream.

Why is it, when you
look at me (a single glance),
I give up my pulse?

Of course, I
can't tell you
'I love you'

Announcing Ourselves

I announce myself
only to you.

You announce yourself
through jokes and glances.

You're a knight of your own survival,
I'm your dragon – conquer me.

Tell me again

tell me again
you love me –

though it sounds
like a cuckoo,
repeating
        again.

Spring doesn't come once but every year
when she brings cuckoos
who nest in her dress.

September haunts me now,
        bring Spring.

Tell me again,
                again,
                              again.

In this moment,
forget crowds:
kiss me.

Our kiss, our kicks, our dance-floor skips,
we laugh, knowing we're not coming back,
halfway between Heaven and the Highway:
Our Way.

Forgetting you

I can't forget
your lips, your skin,
your starlight eyes.

I hide because I need to forget

but I remember
        too well.

Rest

with me
in bed.

Nobody to bother us
with their life-stories.

Live now –
forget past
and future.

Shedding

For once,
remember moments
stripped of rules

when your smile
grows too **big**
for your face

& your heart
beatstoofast
for your chest:

in that moment,
if you find the world
insignificant

it won't matter.

Digital Aubade

You say you hear the alarm clock ping
as its red numbers switch to 8AM.

My pulse is better than digital,
it says 'no need for alarm'.

You want coffee. I shake my head,
my lips still wet with wine.

You claim you see the sun,
it's just streetlights:
their bright electric shine.

You roll over. Holding you, I admit
it's morning, now. Still – let's invert the hours –
get up at 8PM instead –

prolong the night
by gate-crashing
        the day.

Return to Our Island

That summer,
we obsessed
over our romance.

I read you ancient poems
from fat books,
slipped their sentiments
 inside my lines.

Erosion

"We're fools whether we dance or not, so we might as well dance."

- Japanese proverb

Apples

When the world is yours, my darling,
we'll eat fruit under trees.
I'll give you an apple, darling,
we'll kiss in tender breeze.
Sing our happy songs, darling,
try not to talk of death
and I'll give you gifts, my darling
I'll give you my last breath.

Toxic

Your kiss is venom
and I know poison kills –
I don't care.

Your nails are tiger-claws:
I've a death-wish.

Your voice is a siren-call,
I crash on your rock.

Your absence is peace.
Give me war.

Strange to think
of skulls
we'll leave
.dniheb

Acknowledgements

Thank you to my editor, Kate Garrett, for all your help with editing my book.

Thank you to J & D for all your help in listening to the various drafts of my poetry and your advice.
Thank you also for allowing me to read 'Apples' at your wedding.

Thank you to C for your early readings of my Grecian poems last summer.

Thank you to Carole for your blurb and for your advice with my poems.

Thank you to April and Angela for your blurbs.

Thank you to Meg for inspiring the name of my book section: 'How We Lived Then'.

My poems 'Turning Cinders' and 'Erosion' have been previously published in 'Carillon' Magazine and 'Northern Type 51' respectively. Thank you to Graham for allowing me to republish them in this book.

2016 Titles from Three Drops Press

Constellations by Susan Castillo Street
Under-hedge Dapple by Janet Philo
Back to Yesterday by Zoe Broome
There is an island by Johnny Giles
Follow the Stag and Learn to Fly by Anna Percy
The Unicornskin Drum by Stella Bahin
A Sprig of Rowan by Rebecca Gethin
The Darkling Child and Other Stories
      by Catherine Blackfeather
Among the White Roots by Bethany W Pope
The First Greek Tragedy by Cora Greenhill
Lykke and the Nightbird by A.B. Cooper

*Full Moon & Foxglove: An Anthology of Witches
      and Witchcraft* edited by Kate Garrett
Tailfins & Sealskins: An Anthology of Water Lore
      edited by Kate Garrett & Amy Kinsman

www.ingramcontent.com/pod-product-compliance
Lightning Source LLC
Chambersburg PA
CBHW061300040426
42444CB00010B/2448